CONTENTS

INTRODUCTION

THE STORY SO FAR . . .

A recurring theme through the history of health, education and social care for the best part of the 20th century has been how to persuade agencies and professionals to work together so that people's needs can be met in a coherent way.

The frequent and sustained complaint from people who use services and carers has been about the bad experiences and frustrations they have had in trying to find their way around different organisations and different systems to get the help they need.

Successive governments have exhorted health, social care, education, leisure and housing bodies to work together for the overall good of the community and for individuals using services.

The Government has, for the time being at least, stopped short of major organisational change on the grounds that it will *simply create new boundaries and lead to instability and diversion of management effort* *(DoH, 1999).*[1] This leaves us with the same challenge of working against the tide of a cumbersome and imperfect system albeit with some very helpful legislative changes that remove some of the barriers to joint work.

Some people approach partnership working as if it were a tried and tested process, believing that if they follow the instructions they will get a predictable result. In practice, joint working owes more to art than science, relying for its success on creativity and making the most of happenstance. Quite often good things happen (that is, in terms of better services for people) as a result of getting round rules rather than following them.

Much of the energy in successful joint working, therefore, goes into creating the right environment and culture. If we can get this right, joint working becomes 'the way we do things around here'. Opportunities for success become an everyday and spontaneous occurrence. This simple fact also contains one of the reasons why large public sector organisations generally have a poor record with only patchy success in genuine joint working.

Any organisation is interested in its own survival and will naturally follow its own agenda. In the public sector this natural protectiveness is overlaid with professional boundaries and different statutory responsibilities that continue to get in the way of real partnership.

Changing a culture to look outwards and to work in partnership can be one of the biggest challenges for an organisation. Partnership work, by its very nature, puts the needs and wishes of people who use services before organisational needs. A comprehensive and sustained programme of organisation development for this kind of change can be hard to achieve, particularly where there is a dynamic political context that creates a kaleidoscopic background against which the organisation is trying to work.

Such a process of organisation development involves trying to change attitudes, language and behaviour and is reflected in recruitment and induction, staff training and development, policies and procedures. Even where all of this is in place there can still be problems if individual staff do not have regular, clear and constructive guidance and positive monitoring from their managers.

Often change happens as a result of a critical mass of small local successes bubbling up into the organisation's consciousness and gradually shifting the balance of behaviour. This can be very effective, as the energy for change is coming from those people actually receiving and delivering services. The challenge with this kind of development is in getting it taken seriously so that it can be promoted across the organisation. If it doesn't become part of the organisation's agenda it will remain patchy and difficult to sustain when individual champions move on, or different organisational demands take precedence.

These are the realities that anyone tackling partnership working will be facing. Understanding this and working in any way possible to overcome difficulties, or find ways round problems, is the most likely place from which most joint work will be starting. However, we are experiencing a sea-change in joint working. Increasingly, people in leadership roles are coming to the conclusion that effective management includes the wider environment and interfaces with other organisations *as a core part of the business* rather than an added extra.

THE POLICY CONTEXT

This sea-change has also been given strength and direction by the Government's policies for the development of public services. The policy emphasis has changed from the theme of **competition** of the previous era to the theme of **partnership**, with a new '*duty of partnership*' introduced in the 1997 White Paper, *The new NHS: Modern, Dependable* (*Department of Health, 1997*)[2] and a clear emphasis on joint working in the local authority companion piece *Modernising Social Services* (*Department of Health, 1999*)[4]

Some of the main themes of the legislation, guidance and performance measures that are driving change across the public sector are:

- Social inclusion
- Promoting independence
- Prevention
- Building community
- Improving health.

A partnership approach is promoted with health, education, social welfare and employment services required to address these themes jointly.

In practice this means, for example:

- Strengthening consultation and empowerment of patients/service users/ citizens
- Helping people to decide for themselves what they want, who should provide it and how
- Working with local communities to build and support inclusive networks and resources.

Building inclusive communities can only be done in partnership, for example, with both public and independent sector services, local businesses and commerce, local community groups and religious organisations.

The range of development work may include, for example:

- Developing regular and accessible transport
- Improving community safety
- Exploring ways of ensuring that there are a range of local amenities or considering how amenities could be brought to people (eg mobile services)
- Supporting local groups to be as effective as they can be.

These themes are brought together in requirements such as:

☞ **The production of a Health Improvement Programme which must be developed in this broader context**

☞ **Joint Investment Plans which require health and local authorities to agree on how they will invest resources to achieve agreed and joint goals**

☞ **National Service Frameworks which require joint local implementation of national standards and performance criteria**

☞ **National strategies that provide a policy framework**

☞ **Finance (eg Partnership, Prevention and Carers Grant) which requires joint agreement on how resources will be used**

☞ **Primary Care Groups and Trusts with social services and other representation on their Boards**

☞ **National Priorities Guidance for Health and Social Services, which set out individual and joint goals.**

Legislation and policy statements that develop this partnership theme are:

The Health Act 1999[5]

This act removes some of the barriers to joint working. It allows health and social care organisations to pool funds, agree on commissioning arrangements and integrate provision. These new arrangements allow for much more flexibility and are often referred to as the Health Act 'flexibilities'.

The NHS Plan, 2000[31]

This is a plan for reform of the NHS and sets out how Government intends to invest in the NHS and what changes it wants to see. It takes the central push to encourage partnership one stage on from the permissive to the prescriptive. With reference to the Health Act flexibilities, the plan emphasises that: "In future we will make it a requirement for these powers to be used in all parts of the country rather than just some."

The plan also announces the proposal to establish Care Trusts to allow even closer integration of health and social care (see Chapter Two, Partnership Arrangements).

White Paper 2001

This White Paper, Valuing People: A New Strategy for Learning Disability in the 21st Century,[30] outlines the problems and challenges facing learning disability services, a new vision for how things should be and how Government plans to bring about change. There is a continued theme of partnership throughout with, for example:

- A requirement that Learning Disability Partnership Boards are put in place to oversee inter-agency planning and the use of Health Act flexibilities. Membership of these Boards should include senior officers from social services, health bodies, education, housing, leisure, independent providers and employment services. Representatives of people with learning disabilities, carers and people from ethnic minorities must be able to take part as full members.
- Access to some funds dependent on the existence of pooled fund arrangements
- A re-statement that "the Government expects the partnership flexibilities to be used in all parts of the country".
- New powers of intervention under the Health and Social Care Bill to be used where there are "failings in partnership working" to direct the use of partnership arrangements or require a Care Trust to be established.

It seems impossible that anyone in the public sector can have failed to get the message. However, we have yet to see what the medium and longer term effects of these policies and requirements will be on the quality of services and outcomes for people using them. What remains true is that, even with these drivers, the business of achieving real partnership working can be complex and difficult and will require some serious attention if it is to be successful.

HOW TO USE THIS GUIDE

This guide looks at some of the practicalities and realities of partnership working. The content is based on experiences of successes and failures gained in the process of undertaking joint work. It does not have all the answers but hopefully will provide a good practical framework for thinking things through. It should help to highlight the areas that need working on and the questions that need tackling.

The chapters go through various phases of partnership working:

Chapter 1 explores laying the ground and working towards partnership

Chapter 2 looks at the different kinds of partnership arrangements and details of what an agreement might contain

Chapter 3 goes through the process of developing and implementing a joint strategy or Joint Investment Plan and how to involve people in that process

Chapter 4 focuses on partnership work with people with learning disabilities and their families to work out with them what help they need to live their lives. It explores how Community Teams may need to re-think themselves to be fit for the future

Chapter 5 explores the ingredients of successful partnership, how to create and maintain a healthy partnership environment and how to manage change to achieve this

Chapter 6 concentrates on how a partnership approach can be developed to ensure that the right standards and quality are achieved and maintained

These areas of development do not necessarily follow one another sequentially in practice. Some things develop in parallel, and sometimes a stage is reached, for example in developing a joint strategy, where the way that services are commissioned or provided needs to be revisited.

Some examples of practical tools that might be used in partnership work are included in the Appendices.

Note: This guide refers to Joint Investment Plans and Primary Care Groups. In Scotland these are known as Trust Investment Plans and Local Health Care Co-ops respectively.

1. MOVING TOWARDS PARTNERSHIP

WHO ARE THE PARTNERS?

Partnership can be a specific arrangement between two or more organisations (a joint purchasing arrangement between a health authority and a local authority, for example). On the other hand, it could be a broader, looser arrangement between a number of organisations (for example, around a local joint plan). Whatever the context, partnership arrangements need to take account of a range of stakeholders in order to make things happen for people that are in line with the general aims underpinning current policy such as:

- Social inclusion
- Promoting independence
- Prevention
- Building community
- Improving health.

The most important partners are people using services, or potential users of services, their families and carers. Partnership includes people as individuals, but also representative groups such as self-advocacy groups, carers groups and voluntary sector organisations (eg Mencap). Ways of involving and empowering people with learning disabilities and their families are described in Chapter 3, *Developing a Joint Strategy and Joint Plans* and Chapter 4: *Partnership with Individuals and their Families: Re-thinking community teams*.

Other stakeholders to take into account, either in direct formal arrangements, or to be consulted and linked in could be:

- Local authority departments (eg social services, education, leisure, highways and transport etc)
- District or borough councils (particularly housing departments)
- Health authorities
- NHS Trusts
- Primary Care Groups
- Primary Care Trusts
- Independent sector providers
- Education providers
- Employment services
- Local community groups
- Community Health Councils

> Make sure the emphasis is on people with learning disabilities and
> their families as the primary partners
>
>
>
> Identify all the key stakeholders
>
>
>
> Consider how they will be involved

AVOIDING SOME EARLY PITFALLS IN DEVELOPING PARTNERSHIPS

Even with the best of intentions, things can go wrong that prevent developments from happening.

Trying to solve all the problems before proceeding

Progress is likely to be severely hampered if all the solutions are sought in advance in order to try and reach an agreement. It simply is not possible to do this. This kind of approach can sometimes be symptomatic of mistrust and can lead to a decision, after all, to leave things as they are. Indeed, in the case of reluctant partners under pressure to agree, seeking answers to all questions and issues might actually be a strategy for avoiding going down a partnership route.

Any joint agreement is going to involve an element of risk. Assessing and acknowledging those risks and considering ways of minimizing and managing them is a key part of the process. Part of a partnership arrangement will be about agreeing how problems might be resolved over time.

Unrealistic expectations

It is important not to raise expectations that joint arrangements will solve all the problems facing services. If, for example, there is a serious shortfall between demand and available resources, that will remain a fact no matter what joint arrangements are entered into. In those circumstances a realistic expectation would be that joint arrangements could, for example:

- Minimise the effects of resource shortfalls by making better use of resources
- Use what resources there are to provide the services that people who use services and carers say they want
- Help to make the picture clearer and strengthen the case for increased resources by sharing information.

Sometimes officers in senior positions or members get carried away with the idea of joint working, in whatever form, and put pressure on managers to move things on to achieve their vision quickly. Driving ahead too quickly, without ensuring that the critical mass of stakeholders have been involved in the excitement, can mean that decisions are taken that then prove extremely difficult to implement.

Starting from the wrong place

The crucial question to agree on is the nature and scope of joint arrangements that will be acceptable to the partner organisations at the time that agreement is being sought. If the proposal being put forward is seriously out of step with some key leaders it is likely to be rejected in its entirety. This may block the way for more modest steps forward that accumulatively and over time could lead to significant change.

It is possible to start anywhere, even with some differences in values and views and with differing stages of development, as long as the partner organisations:

☞ **Are clear about what it is they are trying to achieve**
☞ **Are honest about their differences and the difficulties they face**
☞ **Are committed to trying to overcome differences and difficulties or find ways round them**
☞ **Are willing to negotiate compromises.**

Whatever the starting point, over time, arrangements can develop and strengthen and provide good foundations for further joint work. By the same token, even the most robust joint arrangements can be undermined by changes in political or senior management commitment. They will be less vulnerable if they have been widely consulted on and have a clear and published programme of development, linked to a joint strategy.

Pandering to the myth of early success

Those entering into partnership arrangements are often under great pressure to demonstrate success quickly.

It is important to emphasize that the goals of partnership are likely to be developmental and incremental. Turning round entrenched attitudes and cultures, or unhappy joint working histories, or building up the right level of resources, does not happen overnight.

It is, nevertheless, a good strategy to try and have some early successes. An example of this would be to ensure that there are some joint or aligned cash budgets that can be quickly accessed to put together services for individuals. Even if these budgets are quite small they can be used to demonstrate the potential for streamlining and using resources creatively.

Identify unanswered questions and agree a process and timescale for addressing them

Base the agreement on realistic expectations

Begin with an achievable agreement that partner organisations feel comfortable with, as a basis for further development

Identify those things that can be achieved early on and those that will take time to develop

PERSUADING PEOPLE IT'S A GOOD IDEA

This is an essential part of the process and the potential for success later on may depend on how well this early work has been done. Firstly, all key people who would need to support a partnership proposal should be identified. It will be helpful to arrange time to talk to key people personally and informally. It is important to cultivate some champions so that they can respond positively when proposals appear in more formal settings.

The proposal should then be taken to people in the form that is appropriate for that forum, for example, reports, presentations, informal discussions, workshops etc.

Forums that will need to support proposals might include:

Advocacy groups, voluntary sector groups, Health Authority Boards, Primary Care Group and Trust Boards, Community Health Councils, local County or Unitary Authority meetings, planning and joint planning forums, health or social care Directorate meetings.

In presenting the proposal material used should:

- Be short and to the point
- Be clear and in plain language
- Concentrate on the benefits for people using services

- Highlight benefits for organisations (such as more streamlined processes and cost effective use of resources)
- Be honest about the risks and challenges but suggest how these could be minimised.

(See Appendix 1 for an example of presentation material)

FINDING THE RIGHT PEOPLE FOR PARTNERSHIP WORK

Developing partnerships is very time-consuming and requires some special skills including:

- Tact
- Diplomacy
- Listening skills
- Flexible thinking
- Interpersonal skills
- The ability to communicate quite complex ideas to a wide audience
- Leadership skills.

It will also need someone with credibility to lead the process who has a sound knowledge and experience of the public sector and how it works.

Quite often, organisations wishing to explore partnership opportunities will create a post, or small unit, specifically to take this development work on. It is not always easy to find someone with this mix of skills and experience. The postholder, often called a Joint Commissioning Manager, or Joint or Partnership Development Manager or something along those lines, can find themselves taking on the world and being expected to resolve all the problems. Sometimes managers are given the job to do in addition to their existing responsibilities. Whoever ends up with the work will inevitably be faced with some potential difficulties.

Some of the tensions they can be faced with are:

- Being disowned by one or other of the partnership organisations who, for example, might make it difficult for them to access information
- Being disowned by both organisations and finding little support for the work in practice
- Being given mixed messages about the commitment to change
- Organisations using the fact of the joint appointment as evidence of joint working and not feeling the need to do much more
- Being expected to do two full-time jobs, one for each organisation eg attending two lots of management and other forums.

In order to minimize these risks the tasks and parameters of the work need to be well defined and expectations from each organisation made clear from the start. There needs to be a formal joint structure at senior level to support the work and ensure that organisational responsibilities for the development of partnership are recognised and undertaken. Lines of accountability to this joint structure and to the reporting bodies of each individual organisation need to be made clear and written in to any agreement.

The path to, and through, partnership, does not run smooth. Recognition of this, and of the ongoing support that people in this role will need, is an important ingredient of success. Joint supervision with identified managers from each organisation can be helpful. It can provide a regular and informal place to discuss tensions and difficulties or talk through ideas and possible solutions.

SUMMARY

Define tasks and expectations

Build in a formal joint structure at senior management level

Clarify lines of accountability and write them into the agreement

Build in personal support for people undertaking partnership work eg joint supervision

2. PARTNERSHIP ARRANGEMENTS

Movement towards some sort of partnership arrangement can be driven from all sorts of directions.

For example:

☞ **Pressure from people using services and carers for organisations to get their act together**

☞ **Something going seriously wrong that could have been avoided with better joint working**

☞ **A critical mass of practitioners pushing ideas into decision-making forums**

☞ **Champions in key places, such as Directors of Social Services or Chief Executives in the health system**

☞ **Local authority or health authority Members seeking change**

☞ **Pressure from central government, for example in the form of performance measures or joint priorities.**

What is not always clear to those driving a joint agenda is that an agreement about partnership work means commitment to putting people who use services, patients, carers, citizens first. It would seem essential, therefore, that those people are fully involved and consulted in reaching that decision, but this is not always the case.

Following on from the Health Act 1999, recent Government guidance *Guidance on the Health Act Section 31 Partnership arrangements* (Department of Health 2000)[5] endorses a consultative approach and outlines ways to improve services with new flexibilities. The partnership arrangements described in the guidance are:

• Pooled funds
• Lead commissioning
• Integrated provision.

However, joint arrangements to work across boundaries and to find better, more streamlined and cost effective ways of doing things, come in all sorts of shapes and sizes.

Cataloguing all the possibilities is not within the scope of this guide. However, there are some broad categories that most arrangements will fall into and some common themes and truths to explore that affect all joint arrangements.

Joint commissioning

A great deal of time and energy can be taken up with trying to agree definitions of joint commissioning. Some discussion can be helpful if it leads to a greater mutual understanding but there is also a danger of becoming *'entangled in fruitless debates about definitions and terms'*. (DoH, 1995)[3] The guidance on joint commissioning published by the Department of Health in 1995 offered a definition of commissioning as:

> **The strategic activity of assessing needs, resources and current services and developing a strategy to make best use of available resources.**

Joint commissioning is therefore when two or more agencies undertake this activity together *'taking joint responsibility for translating strategy into action'*. (BILD, 1996)[25] offers a working definition of joint commissioning as:

> **A process where two or more agencies agree to jointly commit their resources to the delivery of services for individuals within a jointly agreed strategy.**

If this is what it is, how you go about it is another question altogether. These broad definitions embrace a very wide variety of local joint commissioning arrangements.

Arrangements can vary greatly in scope *from*:

* Local joint operational commissioning and joint purchasing of individual packages of care for people with learning disabilities

to:

* Strategic commissioning of all health and social care for community services for all care groups.

There are also a bewildering variety of structural arrangements to deliver joint commissioning, with all shapes and sizes of joint teams for local joint purchasing and all manner of strategic commissioning teams or joint 'agencies'. People sometimes find it difficult to see where comissioning (and therefore joint commissioning) fits in to the scheme of things. This is particularly true in some social services departments where commissioning has not been particularly well developed as an activity.

There should always be a simple process for individuals to access the help they need. However, there is no getting away from the fact that what goes on behind the delivery of even the most straightforward service can be very complex indeed. The overall needs of the total population have to be taken into consideration, budgeted for and accounted for at the same time as services are developed to meet individual needs. Balancing these activities across a complex range of needs and across agencies and organisations requires some careful management. One way to conceptualise this is to see it as three strands of activity that are inter-linked to achieve the required outcomes for individuals: *assessing individual need, commissioning, developing and providing services.*

Partnership for positive outcomes

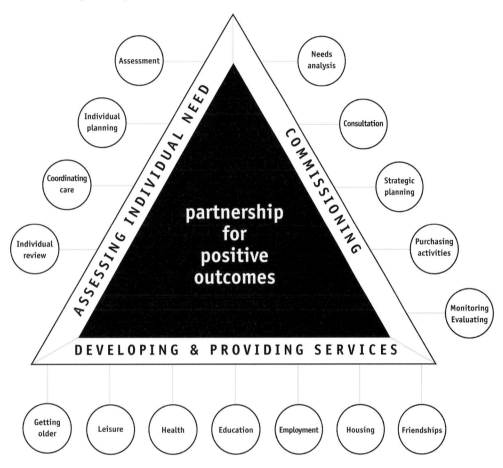

With regard to the commissioning part of this matrix, it is probably most helpful to concentrate on the activities involved in commissioning and to consider which ones are to be included in joint arrangements and to what level of *jointness*. This will inform the kind of structures needed and indicate where work needs to be done to strengthen or develop processes.

The Office of Public Management devised a grid (see overleaf) which shows the different activities involved in commissioning and the stages of development towards *jointness*. This diagram also demonstrates how joint commissioning can develop over time.

TASKS AND LEVELS OF JOINT COMMISSIONING

<— Low level ————————————————————————————————————> High level

Planning and strategic service review	Separate plans, planning and service review processes	Some joint consultation on plans and service reviews	Some agreed overlap of plans and service reviews	Linked plans and service reviews	All plans, service review and planning processes joint
Budgets	Understanding about how much each agency is spending on services	Agencies each earmark budgets or money around a specific project	More monies earmarked for more projects. Budgets aligned	Pooling some part of agencies' main budgets	Pooling of main agency budgets
Contracting/ service agreements	Separate agreements and processes	Joint consultation over specifications	Alignment of processes	Some joint agreements and joint processes	All agreements and contracting processes joint
Management	Separate management arrangements	Meetings of local managers	Joint Lead Project Managers for some specific tasks	Management for some main tasks merged	Joint management arrangements
Consultation	Separate consultation processes where they exist	Joint one-off consultations	Common approaches to consultation adopted	Regular use of joint processes in some consultations	Joint consultations undertaken routinely
Information and systems	Little or no sharing of information	Sharing some information	Some joint information, collection and analysis	Some joint information systems	Joint information systems

(Adapted from a grid devised by the Office of Public Management)

The grid can be a helpful analytical tool to assess where organisations are with regard to joint working, how far they wish to go and which activities will therefore need to be further developed.

Plotting where organisations are on this grid may reveal, for example, that joint planning at a strategic level is well developed, but implementation is hampered by low levels of joint work on finance and contracting.

Lead commissioning
In this arrangement the definition of commissioning remains the same but one agency agrees to take it on *on behalf* of another. This provides a single point for commissioning a range of services.

The same areas of agreement need to be reached with regard to, for example, scope, finance, aims and objectives, but the commissioning arrangements will be integrated into the systems and procedures of the lead commissioning agency.

All agencies entering into a lead commissioning arrangement retain liability for the commissioning they are delegating. The lead commissioning body takes responsibility for actually carrying out the commissioning.

Both partners in this arrangement will need to be clear that, whilst one is acting on behalf of the other, this does not mean that the other partner can opt out of responsibility. Clear and equal responsibilities will need to be built in to the agreement, for example about ringfencing funds or how increases in resources in response to increased demand will be negotiated. It will also be necessary for commissioners acting on behalf of the lead agency to have easy access to information and to continue to be a presence in the systems of both organisations.

JOINT OR INTEGRATED PROVISION

Joint working

Joint working arrangements in services have been developed in a number of areas. The most common arrangements are around community teams of one sort or another. These can have single management structures with workers from one agency seconded in to the managing agency, or have variations of joint management arrangements. Those people not employed by the managing agency, for example, may have professional supervision via their employing agency. Some respite or day services may also have staff from different agencies working together. There are some inherent problems in these arrangements, for example:

- Poor communication
- Differences in perception about roles
- Lack of clarity about aims and objectives
- Conflicts about allocation of work
- Conflicting professional priorities.

These difficulties are overcome with varying degrees of success. Generally speaking, if there is a critical mass of people wanting it to work, it usually will. This can be more by luck than judgement and such arrangements can be fragile and fraught with difficulties.

Integrated provision

Integrated provision under the new Section 31 rules (*Department of Health*, 2000)[5] essentially means providing a service, or a range of services, in an arrangement where different professionals can carry out their work under a single management structure.

Staff in these arrangements may transfer to the provider or be seconded but all staff will work under one management structure. The rules also allow for generic roles to be developed so that one member of staff can be trained to carry out a number of tasks that may previously have been carried out by a range of different staff.

In addition there is a very significant change in the rules to allow either agency to employ both health and social care professionals. This could mean, for example, that an NHS or Primary Care Trust could employ a range of health and social care professionals to provide a comprehensive service. Similarly, a local authority could recruit health personnel to extend the range of a service. The object of these new freedoms is to simplify the ways in which joint work can be delivered by having a genuine single management structure.

Care Trusts

Care Trusts are a new organisational framework for integrated commissioning and provision. Guidance so far indicates that Care Trusts will be in the health system but with local council services delegated through the 1999 Health Act powers.

Care Trusts will bring together staff from the NHS and the local council under one management structure. Such a body could have, for example:

- Joint strategic commissioning responsibilities
- Integrated health and social care teams
- A single pooled budget
- Integrated provision with sheltered housing.

Those people working in multi-disciplinary teams within the same employing NHS Trust could testify to the fact that the difficulties of joint working extend beyond single management. Joint working can suffer the same difficulties within the same organisation. As John Ovretveit has continually pointed out in his work on multi-disciplinary working, a group of staff working within the same organisation does not constitute a team (*Ovretveit, 1993*).[6] Work on attitudes, different approaches and systems, information sharing, culture change etc still need to be tackled, wherever the 'team' finds itself. The advantage of a single management structure is that this kind of development work should be more streamlined and less cumbersome to organise and manage.

JOINT FUNDING

Contributing resources to an agreed service

This form of partnership has been used successfully and creatively to develop services. Where a service need has been identified but it is not possible or appropriate for one agency alone to fund it, each partner agency contributes resources to make it possible for the development to happen. This kind of collaborative funding can be quite complex. A good example of this is the collaborative work around housing with support.

Funding for a special needs housing scheme could be a combination of District Council or Housing Corporation capital for the bricks and mortar with local authority social services revenue for the care element. If some of the residents have been discharged from a long-stay hospital there may also be money from the health authority transferred to social services (under section 28a of the NHS Act 1977) to contribute to the care element.

Joint Funding: Housing

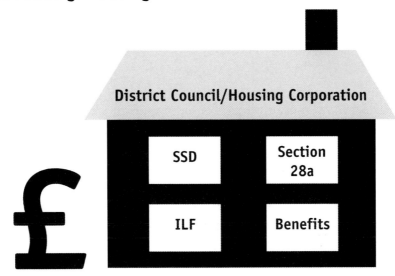

The total cost of care may also be made up of individual contributions from Housing Benefit and other benefits or the Independent Living Fund. People may also be employing their own staff through Direct Payments. Part of the total individual arrangement may also include funding from education sources. Each agency remains responsible for separately identifying, accounting for and auditing their element of the financial package.

Trying to bring all this together successfully can be the cause of premature grey hair for those managers with a co-ordinating role. Unpicking things if there are changes or disputes can also prove difficult. Nevertheless it has been a very successful way of achieving desired outcomes for people.

Pooled Funds
The pooled fund arrangement under the Section 31 arrangements allows different agencies to delegate functions and finance to a joint pool of money and to those authorised to access it. In this way, resources can be brought together to commission a range of services from the same source of funding. This does not absolve partner agencies from their statutory responsibilities but provides a new way to discharge them that will meet people's needs more flexibly.

Once in the pool the money loses its origin and can be used to meet the needs of people using the service regardless of the source and level of funding from each partner. This means that a clear set of aims and objectives, performance measures and outcomes for what the money is intended to buy has to be drawn up. The money is audited as a pooled fund. It is monitored against the joint aims and objectives agreed for the service and outcomes for people who use services.

This helpful step forward means that difficult and sometimes bizarre discussions about what is health and what is social care (and therefore who should pay for it) can be avoided.

One agency has to act as 'host' for the money and a Pool Manager must be identified to have overall responsibility for the fund. Local managers are responsible for managing their delegated part of the pooled fund budget in the normal way.

The partner organisation concerned would be entering into an agreement in which delegation of responsibilities is a key factor. The partners, Members and the Regional Office of the NHS Executive would need to be satisfied that arrangements were robust enough to ensure that:

- Statutory duties are being met
- Aims and objectives for the fund are being met
- Budgets are properly managed and monitored
- Agreements allow for joint decisions about eg service priorities, inflation, efficiency and other savings.

The pool could be around one project, for example:

• •

A person-centred planning approach has identified a need for a service which can offer help for people with very complex needs and their families. The service aims to provide whatever additional assistance people need to live their lives. It is available in a very flexible way that can be adapted to personal requirements. The service provides help at home with daily living, supported holiday options as an alternative to traditional respite care, support for people in employment, leisure and other activities, where it is needed. It also provides support with access to general health care, and where this is appropriate, specialist help with, for example, mobility, communication, mental health, emotional difficulties, managing epilepsy. The service brings together a range of health and social care staff.

• •

The money to support this service is in one flexible pooled fund and is used to fund whatever help is needed.

Arrangements around a relatively small project are likely to be easier to reach agreement about than those on a larger scale. Some areas, particularly where joint working or joint commissioning are well advanced, are likely to want to pool the total investment in health and social care services. Naturally this would be a far more difficult arrangement to agree on. This is not unreasonable given that it might be a £30–£40 million budget.

One way to take this forward to reassure all those concerned would be to start by setting up the joint accounting systems to support the pool but leaving the money in existing budgets with existing budget holders. This would have the effect of rationalizing the money into one system but without actually changing anything in terms of service delivery. Everyone would then have an opportunity to test out the robustness of the system and to ensure that checks and balances are working. Once established, say after a six month period, money could then begin to be moved around, according to plans and needs, into new 'pool' cost centres.

Where services have a strategic framework which has been fully consulted on, this arrangement offers some exciting opportunities for real change where resources could be used creatively and things could be done differently with relative ease.

INFORMAL ARRANGEMENTS

Some joint arrangements are informal and rely on, for example:

- Individual responsibility for behaving jointly
- Good networking
- Communications systems that people have informally agreed to comply with
- Mutually agreed procedures that haven't necessarily been formally adopted
- Informal problem solving forums
- Strong local leaders
- People who get on with each other.

Informal arrangements like this can be very successful and deliver good quality individual services. Hopefully work like this will continue no matter what organisational arrangements have been entered into or however poor collaboration between agencies is elsewhere in the system.

The strengths of this informality are also its weaknesses. Things can change quite quickly if the people involved change and it can lead to quite dangerous collapses of communication if things go wrong.

MIXED ARRANGEMENTS

These arrangements can be used together in different combinations. Joint commissioning and lead commissioning can also have joint provision as part of the range of options available for services. There may also be some pooling of budgets within this combination of arrangements. However, there may be some limitations on combining lead commissioning and pooled funds if those funds represent the majority of funding for a care group. This might be perceived as rather too many eggs in one partnership basket and begins to look more like a single system than a partnership arrangement.

NHS or Primary Care Trusts may enter into a full joint provision arrangement (for example, by forming a single Trust to deliver the full range of services). Depending on how much provision still remains within statutory services, this could look like a single provider monopoly that might not offer the kind of flexibility needed for really responsive services and could be a way of protecting the status quo. In a way, such an arrangement needs to build into its agreement a 'self-destruct' policy that allows for the prospect of organisational change and the diversification of services. Some newly reconstituted NHS Trusts have had to take this healthy and pragmatic stance in the light of possible Primary Care Trust developments.

WHICH OPTION?

The kind of arrangement that develops is going to depend on where people are locally. Ideally, partnership should come out of a mutual desire to achieve the best and most cost effective services for the local population. However, there are a number of factors that might encourage or discourage partnership, which may affect the steps to joint working that can potentially be taken or the state of readiness to take on a new way of working.

Some factors might be, for example:

☞ **The local history of joint working:**
   – Is there a history of good joint working?
   – Have joint working relationships been fragile (or in some cases actually hostile?)
   – Is joint commissioning fully developed or in development?

☞ **Self advocacy:** The strength of the voice and development of local self-advocacy and campaigning groups

☞ **The stage of hospital closure:**
   – Is it all done and dusted?
   – Is it still underway?
   – Has it been complete for so long the reprovision is now being reviewed?

☞ **Politics**
- Are local authority Members, health authority Members, NHS Trust or Primary Care Group/Trust Boards likely to be sympathetic to joint projects? Or are they preoccupied with internal change?
- Will they want to take the opportunity for change or not really want to rock the boat?
- Are local elections due? This can take local authorities into a 'no banana skins' mentality which holds up service development.
- Is there a broader organisational change, for example in county council structure or re-configuring Trusts, or in the light of developing Primary Care Trusts, that is going to have a knock-on effect on how services for others are commissioned and provided?

☞ **The size and nature of existing services**
- How are services made up locally? Are the majority of services in the independent sector? Are substantial services still provided by statutory services? If so, what is the health/social care balance?

☞ **Geography**
- Are services concentrated in a large urban area or dispersed across a rural area? Or a mixture of both?

☞ **Best Value reviews**
- What recommendations for change have been made or are likely to emerge?

Examples of how developments into partnership arrangements, in reality, might be triggered are, for example:

- a natural progression from work that has already been underway such as joint commissioning or joint purchasing arrangements, or work on a joint strategy
- a desire on the part of commissioners or local authority Members to make some substantial changes to move things on because they are not happy with the way existing services are being delivered (this might come out of the result of a Best Value review)
- as a result of organisational change elsewhere in the system.

EXAMPLE

A County Council is re-organising in line with the Government's Modernising agenda. It is streamlining its departments and has decided to merge the children's part of a social care service with its education department. Residential and home care services have already been transferred to the independent sector, so only mental health and learning disabilities in-house social care provision remain. There may be a strong political agenda, therefore, for this remaining social care provision to be merged into joint provision within the health system. This may or may not be in line with agreed values and principles about where services should most appropriately be placed. Consultation would need to thoroughly test out the views of other stakeholders on this.

••

All of these things will influence decisions about the approach that will be taken in developing partnership.

WHAT'S IN AN AGREEMENT?

A partnership agreement provides the framework for the way organisations have resolved to behave with each other. It cannot answer all the questions that are likely to come up. It is unlikely, however long and legal looking it appears, that a written agreement will stop either organisation reneging on or sabotaging the deal if they decide to do so.

Partnership can only work on mutual trust and an agreement should reflect this. It can provide clarity about the nature and parameters of the partnership arrangement and what should happen if things go wrong. A clear, simple agreement that people will read and understand is likely to be more easily arrived at and more useful than a lengthy, wordy document full of quasi-legal language that creates more confusion than clarity. Partners need to decide on a framework for what they think would be useful to write down and sign up to.

Some of the things that might be included are:

☞ **Who are the parties to the partnership arrangement?** This would be those directly involved and include reference to people who would be linked in (eg housing departments)

☞ **Principles of the partnership** eg Commitment to consultation and involving people, to the implementation of joint plans and strategies, to build on trust and openness to resolve problems, to share financial information etc

☞ **Who is it for?** Which service user group or groups does it cover?

☞ **What is it for?** What is the nature of the partnership arrangement and how it can be described eg a Pooled Fund, social services in a lead commissioning role etc

☞ **What organisational arrangements will exist to support it?** Eg posts, lines of accountability, reporting forums, joint executive bodies, steering group, Member support etc

☞ **What is the scope of the agreement?** What services, specifically, will be included in the arrangement and what legal and statutory frameworks, if any, cover them?

☞ A statement about resources
  – What is each organisation committing to the partnership agreement: flexible budgets? existing services? posts?
  – Will the resources be ring-fenced?
  – Which services will carry a charge to people using them?
  – Agreement on the process to consult one another about efficiency and other savings
  – Arrangements about the process for negotiating resources to meet increases in demand or planned developments
  – Financial and budget management arrangements
  – Delegated budget arrangements
  – Preventing and addressing overspends
  – Carry forward of underspends
  – Inflation
  – Forecasting and reporting to contributing partners

☞ The process for resolving disputes

☞ Information sharing. What has been agreed about this? Who will have access to what information? Will there be shared records?

☞ Assessment and care management arrangements

☞ Governance eg business planning, openness of appointments, complaints, standards of behaviour, independent review, conflicts of interest etc

☞ Exit strategy. What happens if either or both parties wish to withdraw. This might include:
  – a commitment to demonstrate that genuine attempts to resolve problems have been made (if it is the result of difficulties)
  – a commitment to fully explain the reasons and to examine the consequences for people using services
  – who needs to give approval and how?
  – what period of notice is required?

Look at the available options

Analyse the local situation, make sure all the possible factors are considered

Take account of national and central government factors eg National Strategies, Service Frameworks, Performance Measures. Look at what is happening elsewhere and learn from their experiences, successes and failures

Carry out an additional appraisal: what are the advantages, disadvantages and possible consequences of each option? Involve people who are good strategic and creative thinkers, who could help describe different and better ways of doing things

Consult with all the stakeholders on possible options

Draw up an agreement that is simple and in plain English

Make sure the agreement makes clear, for example: who it's for, what it's for, organisational arrangements, the scope, resources committed, process for resolving disputes, information sharing, assessment and care management arrangements, governance, exit strategy.

3. DEVELOPING A JOINT STRATEGY AND JOINT PLANS

THE RIGHT APPROACH

Any Principal or Policy Officer worth their salt could sit down and write a joint strategy, tapping in to various information sources and their own knowledge and experience of what constitutes good practice and good services. They might gather together a few representatives from different agencies and from parts of the learning disability community to help them. They could probably deliver a substantial document in a matter of months. The result might read very well and be much admired.

This approach is likely to run into serious problems, not to mention brick walls, when those promoting it need to turn it from strategy into action to achieve goals, win resources and change services. The development of a joint strategy that will be significant for all those involved in using, commissioning or providing services is likely to be a long and decidedly more painful process.

It is vital that, throughout the process, people with learning disabilities are enabled to participate. Ken Simons' book *A Place at the Table* (BILD, 1999)[7] offers some very helpful advice on how to ensure that people can participate. He argues the case that participation:

> ☞ **Is a moral imperative:** it is a fundamental part of being a citizen and the role of services is to help enable people to be full citizens
> ☞ **Makes for better services:** services that have taken into account people's wishes are more likely to be focused on the reality of people's lives
> ☞ **Can mean greater protection:** abuse can happen where there is a culture of compliance (*Craft, 1996*)[8] and greater dependence on staff.
> ☞ **Can have a positive impact on the self-esteem of people with learning disabilities:** people are likely to feel better about themselves if they have been encouraged to be more confident and assertive, make choices and have more control.

Depending on what state of jointness and consensus already exists, a joint strategy that engages the whole learning disability community could take up to two years to fully develop. This will be hard for those who want quick fix results to live with. It may seem like an unnecessarily long process but it is at the heart of the development of real partnership to bring about real change.

This does not mean that short term action to achieve positive gains cannot be made at every stage on the way.

In the process of developing a joint strategy, key partnership activities will take place such as:

- Building relationships
- Engaging positively with people who use services and carers
- Building clear pictures of what is already available
- Arriving at a consensus and describing what is needed.

LISTENING TO PEOPLE

As many people as possible should be engaged in discussion and in as many different ways as possible.

Some of the questions that will need to be addressed are, for example:

- What is currently invested in services and how that is used
- What kind of assistance people want and need to live their lives
- How services should be set up to respond to this
- What changes would need to be made to existing services to achieve this
- How people will work together to achieve this.

If these discussions are going to be fruitful they may also involve acknowledging and working on some of the real tensions that exist, for example:

- The tension between what carers may express as their view of the way things should be and the way people with learning disabilities see things
- Differences in view or values between professionals within the same organisation and between organisations
- Some significant variations in views or values between self-advocacy and voluntary or watchdog organisations (such as Community Health Councils, Mencap, People for People)
- Complexities in the political view that might influence, say, whether or not services should or should not be provided by statutory agencies.

In addition to these differences between different parts of the community, there will not be a single view from any one part. Carers, for example, will not have a single view of the way things should be. There will be a range of views from each part of the community.

All these views will need to be balanced carefully. This is not going to be easy and will need to be well thought through. It is important for reasons to be given for decisions taken. Some people may not agree with some decisions, but they should have participated and should have been informed about the rationale for decisions. Rating or scoring systems can be used in consultation but this should not be too simplistic. Choosing an option which suits the

Listen to *me* . . .

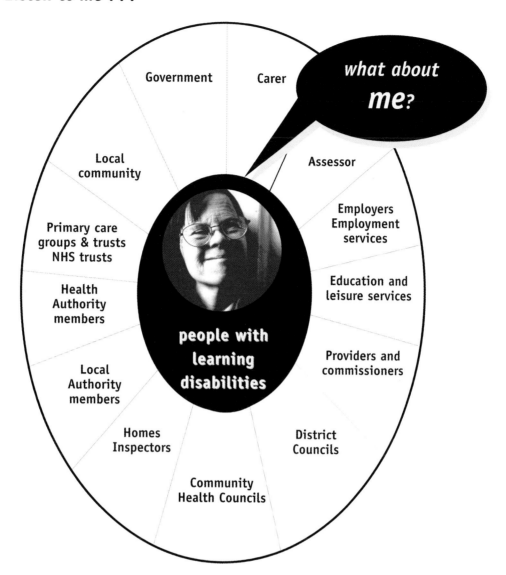

views of the largest number of people may discriminate against minorities and people who may want something different. Plans will need to reflect a range of views and options. *Joint Investment Plans: A learning disabilities workbook* (*DoH 2000*)[29] discusses ways of prioritizing, such as risk analysis techniques that look at the consequence of not doing something. However it is tackled, the process involved in deciding on service development options and priorities should be clear and open.

Focusing on outcomes

In order to keep on track it is important to start by considering outcomes for people rather than diving immediately into the way services should look. This will also ensure that agencies are focusing on needs first rather than service solutions.

General areas of need to focus on that emerge might be:

Aspects of living:	In support of this:
Leaving school	Rights, advocacy and involving people
Somewhere to live	Assessing need and co-ordinating care
Education	Skills training
Leisure	The nature of support and assistance needed (eg
Employment	personal care)
Health	Support for carers
Friendships and relationships	Promoting diversity
Getting older	Quality assurance
	Human resource and workforce development

A CONSULTATION PLAN

A consultation plan should involve a number of methods of engaging with people. The idea is to get as many different views in as many different ways as possible.

If there is a specific learning disability focus in the joint planning system then this would be a useful forum to lead and own the process. The new Partnership Boards for Learning Disability Services should have a key role in leading on consultation.

A consultation plan might include:

- Workshops or conferences with one part of the community (eg service users)
- Workshops or conferences with mixed participants from different parts of the community
- Surveys to reach those people who can't or are disinclined to participate in events
- Use of existing networks and forums – this could be by assisting with finance or support for people to have their own events, or by attending their meetings and forums to seek views
- Supporting advocacy services (either local or national, if local advocacy services are not yet fully developed). This could be financially or, for example, by providing other assistance so that people with learning disabilities can directly consult other people with learning disabilities.

If it is not to be tokenistic some serious thought needs to go in to how people will be engaged in consultation exercises.

People who have apparently been consulted complain, for example, that

- They have been given not enough or too much information
- Information doesn't make sense to them

- there has not been openness and honesty in the process
- they are not being listened to
- consultation events are sometimes dominated by the opinions of a few very vocal people and they haven't had a chance to have their say
- they don't get to hear what difference the consultation made, if any.

Some simple rules are:

Involving people

▶ Be clear about what it is you are asking people to do:
  - comment on a proposal that is being put to them?
  - listen to a range of options and express preferences?
  - express their own views and ideas about how existing services could be changed?
  - express views and ideas about how services could be in the future?

▶ If you are bringing people together for an event:
  - make sure there is a good balance between listening and the opportunity to participate
  - break up discussion so that it could be, for example, in pairs, round the table, in workshop groups
  - be clear about the specific task you are giving people in groupwork
  - make sure views are recorded

▶ Give everyone an opportunity to have their say by:
  - going round the group asking each individual to make a comment so that one or two people don't hog the discussion
  - having a 'talking wall': give people stickers to write their comments on during the day to stick up on the wall. This gives them a chance to say things they may not have been able to say directly.

▶ Set up 'stalls' with pictures and information and someone who can explain what the stall is about. This gives people an opportunity to have a one-to-one discussion about things. You can also give people stickers to attach to different stalls to indicate their support or preferences. This technique was used successfully at a conference for people with learning difficulties to help prioritise what was most important to them. The stall with the most stickers indicated what most people felt was most important

▶ Follow the rules for good presentations. Use large bold lettering, not more than about seven lines of text. Use colour, pictures and diagrams to make things interesting and keep people engaged

▶ Avoid the token appearance of senior managers. Often they appear at the beginning of an event, give their presentation and rush off to their next (more important?) appointment. Managers should be there to *listen* as well as give information or explanations. Listening will involve spending time with people during the day

▶ Be open and honest with people, for example, about resources, the quality of services, what has already been agreed and is not really negotiable

- ▶ Make sure people have feedback about what people said and what has happened as a result of the consultation

- ▶ If things haven't happened, explain why

Using questionnaires and surveys
- ▶ If you are using questionnaires and surveys:
  - be clear about the limitations: it will present another opportunity to get a good idea of the way people think and feel about things but it is not the whole story
  - don't be too ambitious: keep it short, otherwise people will be inclined not to bother
  - use reply-paid envelopes
  - make sure people are clear about why the survey is being carried out and what will happen to the results
  - keep questions simple, with short sentences and good grammar. Use tick boxes wherever possible and if you have to use jargon, explain what it means
  - use some open-ended questions
  - if you gather information in a haphazard way it may be difficult to make sense of: one way to help with this is to design the survey so that it has a range of statements – give people the opportunity to express the extent to which they agree or disagree and what priority they would give to things
  - make sure people are clear about confidentiality and can have the option of remaining anonymous if they wish
  - give people an opportunity to add their own views about areas that were not covered

- ▶ If you are designing a questionnaire for people with learning disabilities:
  - work with people with learning disabilities to design it and test it out
  - use font size 14 as people may be able to read text in a larger font
  - use some pictures eg The Change Picture Bank (See Appendix 2)
  - use smiley faces so that people can express their approval/disapproval.

Joint Investment Plans

The same principles and methods apply to the development of a Joint Investment Plan. Health and local authorities, together with their partners, are required to develop Joint Investment Plans. For general guidance see the *Guidance on Joint Investment Plans* issued by the Department of Health. Joint Investment Plans are three year programmes to support the delivery of key aspects of the Health Improvement Programme. The purpose of these joint plans is to:

- Facilitate greater integration between the NHS, social care, housing and other key agencies
- Achieve transparency in respective health and local authority investment in continuing and community care by charting this systematically
- Establish strategic goals and priorities
- Produce the information necessary to support the reshaping of services across the health and social care economy.

If a Joint Strategy has already been developed this will feed in to the Joint Investment Plan. The Department of Health has produced some guidance specifically for the development of Joint Investment Plans for services for people with learning disabilities (*Joint Investment Plans: A learning disabilities workbook, Department of Health, 2000*).

Implementing joint strategies and plans

Having consulted comprehensively the next stage is to draw up a clear strategy in plain English. A joint strategy should not set out to answer all the questions, but it should:

- give a clear value base and principles on which services should be based
- give an overview of current services and resources
- set out aims and objectives for services agreed in the consultation process
- say what process for action is needed to make things happen
- provide milestones and a measure for achievement of aims and objectives over a defined period of time.

JOINT PROJECT PLANNING

If a strategy is not to sit on the shelf gathering dust, a robust joint project planning system should be developed to deliver the aims and objectives. At first this may seem to have a touch of bureaucracy, but with such a large agenda for action, it is vital that there is a way of organising and monitoring the work. In the absence of project management, implementation may happen in a haphazard way or not at all.

The project management process:

- should be owned at the highest level in the partnership organisations in the form of a Joint Project Management Board
- should have a full time project manager
- should have dedicated help from support services in each organisation to ensure that realistic costings, financial and workforce plans are developed
- have an agreed budget to cover the cost of, for example, cover for people who are involved in task group work, consultation, publishing information in accessible forms, administrative support etc

Without these elements in place the implementation process is unlikely to be effective.

A project structure should be agreed that divides the work up into task groups with clear objectives and timescales for achieving them. The structure of task groups will depend on what work and priorities have been identified. It is best not to generate too many groups.

A typical structure might be, for example:

- ▸ Housing with support
- ▸ Leisure, employment and education
- ▸ Personal relationships
- ▸ General health
- ▸ Involving people/accessible information
- ▸ Assisting individual communication
- ▸ Children, families and transition
- ▸ Support for carers.
- ▸ Promoting diversity.

Each of these groups should be empowered to commission work as necessary. However the tasks are divided up, it is important to plan in links that acknowledge the overlaps, and give consideration to how the links will be made. One way of doing this is to ensure that there are regular meetings with all project leads to share information.

Task groups should report regularly to the Joint Project Management Board. The Board has a co-ordinating role:

- Making sure that communication links between task groups are made
- Agreeing on or seeking resources in support of implementation
- Reporting regularly to joint planning forums
- Communicating progress to all stakeholders.

Project management tools should be developed for consistency so that, for example:

- Risk assessments for the proposed action can be carried out
- Specific aims and objectives for tasks and action plans are made clear
- Reporting mechanisms give the right kind and level of information
- The way work is carried out conforms to the values and principles that underpin the strategy (eg involving people at all stages).

Be aware that developing a joint strategy or Joint Investment Plan that involves genuine participation will take time and careful planning

Make sure that people with learning disabilities are enabled to participate throughout the process: take advice on this if necessary

Focus on outcomes: don't jump into service solutions

Draw up a consultation plan that outlines all the different ways that people can be involved

Be clear what it is you are asking people to do in the consultation process: be honest about things eg resources and what is, or is not, negotiable

Report back to people the conclusions of consultation

Explain why you are, or are not, going to do things

Produce a clear joint plan in plain English, produced in different accessible versions

Ensure that there is a well-planned project management process to deliver the plan

4. PARTNERSHIP WITH INDIVIDUALS AND THEIR FAMILIES: RE-THINKING COMMUNITY TEAMS

WHERE WE'VE COME FROM

Before looking at potential partnership arrangements between individuals and specialist professionals, it might be helpful to see where we have come from.

Many Community Learning Disability Teams (or Community Mental Handicap Teams as they were once called) came into being as part of the wave of development around hospital closure programmes in the 1980s. They were often central to service development and innovation as well as working in whatever way necessary to get services for individuals sorted out and to supply whatever support or therapeutic interventions they were able to. They were generally the main source of information and help.

These teams were various in their arrangements but were usually made up of a mixed bag of professionals trying to work together to the same ends, with social workers and community nurses as core members. They were certainly not without their tensions and problems and struggled with these as all multi-disciplinary and multi-agency projects do. However, they were responsible for much innovation and development. Some of the good practice that went on in these teams informed the thinking that led to the 1991 NHS and Community Care Act. Ironically, as far as Community Learning Disability Teams were concerned, this Act, rather than helping to overcome problems and aid development, had the effect of a bowling ball hitting skittles and seemed to send teams flying off in all directions.

The Act placed a lead responsibility for assessment and care management on local authority social service departments, with health professionals having a responsibility to contribute to the process. The new arrangements also involved the notion of separating the functions of assessment and care management on the one hand from provision on the other. This also involved transforming some social workers (or all social workers, depending which model you were in) into a newly conceived role as *care managers*.

The result was a proliferation of structural responses for much of the joint working around services for people with learning disabilities. Professionals found themselves dispersed in diverse arrangements as agencies struggled with who was supposed to do what in the new world of purchasers and providers.

The reality that faces us now is that this diversity is likely to continue, for example with teams being affected by the development of Primary Care Trusts and developments in integrated provision resulting from some of the 1999 Health Act opportunities and the White Paper.

Pick 'n mix community teams

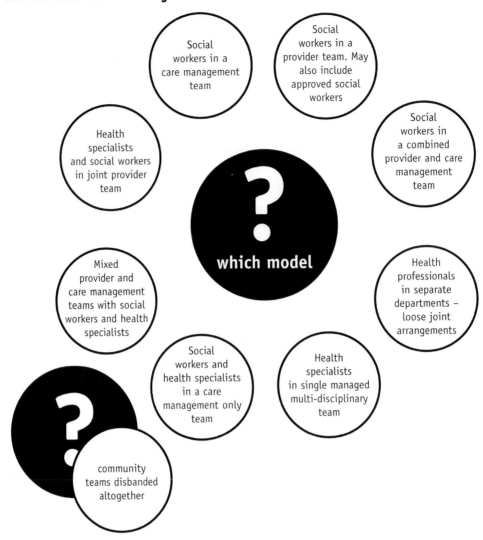

Where they continue to exist, Community Teams are likely to still be configured in a variety of ways, whoever employs them. This means that unless some focus is given to teams they will still suffer from some of the negative effects of the post-Community Care Act changes, for example:

- Confusion over roles and responsibilities
- Lack of direction
- Erosion of some professional skills
- A sense of disempowerment as individual workers
- The threat of being decommissioned in the face of other priorities.

GETTING ON TRACK

In their article *Is there a future for the Community Learning Disabilities Team? (Greig R, Peck E, 1999)*[9] Rob Greig and Edward Peck give a very helpful account of these historical changes and their effects and a warning that:

'. . . if the teams are to continue, albeit in an evolved role, then they have to be able to offer a purpose for their existence.'

In order to survive, and survive in a form that is going to be useful to people with learning disabilities and their families, specialist health and social care professionals may need to ask themselves some fundamental questions. For example:

- What difference would it make in the lives of people with learning disabilities and their families if we were not here? And, therefore, what positive differences can we make?
- How can we demonstrate this in a clear way?
- What changes do we need to make to ensure that we continue to be useful in ways that the people we're there to help want us to be (eg changes in attitude, behaviour, and ways of functioning).

Being focused and keeping on track may involve, for example:

- Developing appropriate ways of working in partnership with people with learning disabilities and their families
- Sorting out core functions and being clear what's on offer
- Focusing on access to services that we all use and supporting community services
- Making sure life outcomes for people as a result of help given are measured and made known
- Developing cultures and attitudes that embrace genuine partnership working
- Being prepared to change the way you do things in response to outcome evidence and feedback from people's experiences.

ASSESSMENT AND CARE MANAGEMENT

One of the core functions of specialist health and social care professionals has been to work together to give a comprehensive assessment of people's needs and to arrange and co-ordinate the help that they need.

These processes of assessment and care management are often not very clearly defined. People sometimes have very different perceptions of what the processes are for and how they are being carried out.

Typically, the process involves:

- The assessment of need
- The development of options for the right services
- Arranging services
- Co-ordinating all the elements of assessment and care management

- Reviewing how effective services are for the person concerned
- Arranging changes in service that have been identified through review or that have unexpectedly arisen.

All specialist health and social care professionals have a role in this process either as co-ordinators or contributors or both. However, they are often unclear both about how the process is actually taking place and what their role is in it. Who does what, whereabouts in the system and how it all fits together is not always clear to everyone concerned.

Comments and findings from a report from the Social Services Inspectorate, based on a series of inspections, *Moving into the Mainstream* (*Social Services Inspectorate, 1998*)[12] and *Facing the facts* (*Department of Health, 1999*)[11] a study of 24 local authority areas, give some clear messages for specialist professionals and the organisations that employ them about the way things are currently done.

Moving into the Mainstream emphasised that assessment and care management was best where carried out in joint health and social services teams in a multidisciplinary way. However, *Facing the Facts* pointed out that only half of the authorities in the study carried out had agreed a protocol to co-ordinate care management across health and social services. Other points made in *Moving into the Mainstream* were:

- Harmonising assessment, care planning and care management across generic and specialist services, across purchaser/provider boundaries and across agencies was proving difficult and in some places the issues had not been addressed
- Many care plans were incomplete, lacking a whole life approach and not making clear the links between required outcomes and services
- User involvement in assessment and care planning was increasing but both service users and carers were often insufficiently involved.

The White Paper[30] confirms that:

'Care management will continue to be the formal mechanism for linking individuals with public services.'

It emphasises, however, that this must now be carried out with a person-centred approach. Further guidance on person-centred planning will be issued to clarify what this means in practice. It will involve a change in the style, approach and power balance in the process and in relationships with people with learning disabilities and their families. For some professionals, this will mean a fundamental change in attitude, language and ways of going about things.

A PERSON-CENTRED APPROACH

What is a person-centred approach?

Partnership with people themselves and their carers is the most important plank of joint working. One way that this can be developed is through a person-centred approach.

The term covers a range of approaches to individual planning that is led by people with learning disabilities and their families and friends. Approaches include: Personal Futures Planning (*O'Brien, 1987*)[10] and Essential Lifestyle Planning (*Smull M and Harrison B, 1992*)[13] and Circles of Support (*Wertheimer A, 1995*).[14] These differ in their detail, but essentially the approach is one of development rather than one-off assessment. The main characteristics in these approaches are that people work together to:

- Form an action group or circle of support which will work collaboratively to help someone
- Share experiences of someone's history, relationships, choices, dreams and Knowledge of what does and does not work for them
- Work out a desirable future and identify obstacles and opportunities
- Work out who they need to enlist in the family, in services or in the community to bring about changes, to create opportunities or to overcome obstacles
- Work out strategies and plans to get there
- Keep on working together in this way and learning.

These approaches also share a set of common beliefs:

> ☞ The primary authorities on the life of someone with a learning disability are the person themselves and those who know and love them. Information from formal assessments is helpful but should be in the context of the account given by the person and/or those closest to them. This turns a typical professional assessment process round the other way
>
> ☞ The purpose of person-centred planning is learning by doing things together. It encourages people to try things together and learn from their experience. It also provides a way of negotiating about conflicts where there are disagreements about what is possible or desirable
>
> ☞ The focus is on enlisting community members to assist in working towards desired outcomes for people and to overcome low or narrow expectations of what might be possible
>
> ☞ It contains a challenge to services not to separate people or perpetuate relationships of controlled dependence
>
> ☞ It is a process that has respect and equality at its heart
>
> ☞ It addresses emotional and ethical issues and encourages the continuing search for effective ways to deal with barriers and conflict.

At first sight it may seem that good conventional individual programme planning or assessment and care management approaches would aspire to do the same things and are therefore not significantly different. In practice there is a fundamental difference in style and approach. No matter how we may choose to wrap it up, a typical professional process usually involves some sort of assessment or measurement, often in a tick-box format, followed by a look at available options, agreeing on an option and then monitoring the fit.

Relationships within the professional process may be very good, but the power is always balanced towards the 'assessor'. A person-centred approach is less linear and requires a more equal balance, breaking down some of those power barriers. The process works on strengthening people's networks and alliances rather than replacing them with 'services'. It involves working hard on clarifying people's individual interests and needs and working together to find new ways of meeting them. Professional assessments *contribute* to this process but do not *drive* it.

It is not hard to see why all this can represent a real threat to some professionals and the organisations that employ them. This approach is particularly powerful if it is alongside an active Direct Payments system where people also have more control over decisions about how money is spent on the help and assistance they need. It happens largely outside of organisational control and can provide a strong and more equal basis for negotiation about access to services and resources. Service systems would need to actively support this by helping people to get started and by being responsive and willing to change their attitudes and ways of doing things.

This would mean some real commitment to training and development strategies for all concerned, both in person-centred planning as a process and in terms of developing a healthy environment for partnership working (see Chapter 5).

In an article describing the King's Fund Changing Days project, Andrea Whittaker and Barbara McIntosh (*Whittaker A and McIntosh B, 2000*)[15] point out that some people with learning disabilities participating in the project were relying to such a great extent on formal services (particularly long-stay patients or ex-patients) that they had mostly paid staff in their lives. The planning circles they set up were therefore not all of a pure circle of support model, but nevertheless they were clear about aims and processes and were aiming to extend the circles as people became more connected in their communities. This would at least be a way of getting things moving in those circumstances. The essential steps of the process they used were:

- Identify the people who you are going to work with
- Agree who is to be the facilitator for each person's planning circle
- Hold a training day for facilitators to go through the overall process and explain the preliminary work needed on collecting information
- The person, with help from their facilitator if necessary, chooses people to be members of their planning circles

- Hold the first planning circle
- Complete the person-centred plan including agreeing on long-term goals and who will support the person, if necessary, to achieve them
- Agree on the next circle meeting
- Review achievements and re-define goals if necessary.

For those people in areas where this kind of approach still seems to be at the end of a long dark tunnel, one place to start might be at least to work with people with learning disabilities on a self assessment process as the starting point for the formal process (see Appendix 2).

The role of assessors/care managers

This kind of partnership approach requires people to use their professional expertise in a different way. Instead of being used to *carry out* assessments, expertise is used to enable others to contribute to the assessment process in a variety of ways. This involves *giving away* different assessment responsibilities and tasks to others, for example:

- To people themselves and their families as self-assessors
- To non-professional service brokers working on behalf of people with learning disabilities and their families
- To providers, who have previously been distanced from the assessment process.

Some people have always been uncomfortable with the term *care manager* because of the implied relationship between those who need the care and those who are apparently 'managing' it. Perhaps we should now consider a new way of describing the role that reflects the need to act as the link between **someone with learning disabilities, their family and friends and those who know them** and **service systems and funding sources**. This function implies *interpreting* and *navigating* rather than managing.

The care co-ordinating role then involves, for example:

- Bringing all the assessment ingredients together
- Acting as interpreter and navigator to help people get what they need from different organisations
- Negotiating with providers to do things in the way that the person and those who know them think will help best
- Helping people to access the financial resources they need.

SPECIALIST HEALTH SERVICES

Person-centred and partnership approaches that promote policies of social inclusion, prevention, promoting independence and building community, also need to be reflected in specialist health services.

Signposts for Success (NHS Executive, 1998)[16] highlighted the extent to which people with learning disabilities are failing to have their health needs met and the role of specialist services in helping to change this. The guidance makes clear that:

People with learning disabilities and their families need access to ordinary services and resources such as health centres, housing and leisure centres, in the same way as other people living in the community, with specialist services providing additional support and services where necessary.

This was followed by *Once a day (NHS Executive, 1999)*[17] which looks at what primary health teams can do to address this. There is a clear role described for health specialists in supporting primary health teams. Similarly there is a role in ensuring that general hospital and other 'mainstream' services (eg mental health services) are sensitive and responsive to the needs of people with learning disabilities.

In other words, specialist health professionals have a role in ensuring that people with learning disabilities are included and have access to the full range of services available to everyone. This involves working directly with the person concerned and their families and with staff and managers, for example:

- Working with someone and those close to them, to prepare them for what they are likely to expect when receiving treatment
- Supporting them through the experience by, for example, explaining things and ensuring that they understand what is happening and what will happen next
- Giving advice to other professionals and staff about this person's particular needs or way of communicating
- Offering specific training to people with learning disabilities, staff or families
- Offering expert assistance, for example in working with someone's potentially violent or self-harming behaviour
- Helping other parts of the health system to develop inclusive policies and staff development and training plans.

What is less clear is what '*additional support and services*' are and specialist health services will need to be clear about what this means and what they can offer, as discussed earlier in this chapter in *Getting on track*.

The White Paper[30] develops the themes outlined in Signposts for Success.[16] It emphasises a shift in balance:

- To provide high quality specialist expertise

- To give more time to facilitating the work of others in mainstream services and less to direct interventions
- To have a key role in supporting people to access mainstream services.

Specialists will need to be able to answer the questions:

- What positive difference can we make in people's lives?
- What outcomes will result from what we do?
- How well are we working with each other and with our partners?
- How person-centred and empowering are our processes, approaches and attitudes?
- How effective are we at helping people to access mainstream services?
- How well do we support community services to be effective?

It may be helpful to carry out a review of how well teams are performing in response to these questions.

In one area a check list was used to review the effectiveness of multi-disciplinary working (see Appendix 3).

It is important to get on to a positive track by identifying action in order to build on good work and maintain it, and to get work underway quickly to address gaps and team development.

Give community teams focus by asking key questions eg What positive difference can we make in people's lives?

Develop appropriate ways of working with people with learning disabilities and their families such as person-centred planning

Develop ways of measuring life outcomes for people as a result of help given

Work actively to develop cultures that embrace a genuine partnership approach, rather than just expecting them to happen

Be prepared to change the way you do things in response to feedback

Be prepared to give away some responsibilities, tasks and power and legitimise this by being responsive to what happens outside of organisational control

Act as an *interpreter* or *navigator* rather than a *care manager*

Help people use their existing supports and access general services and be clear about what specialist services are for, where these are needed and used

Check out how well teams are performing and agree on action for development

5. DEVELOPING AND MAINTAINING A HEALTHY PARTNERSHIP ENVIRONMENT

INGREDIENTS OF SUCCESSFUL PARTNERSHIP

There are some essential ingredients that make up a healthy environment and culture for partnership working. Quite often organisations focus attention on the systems and processes that make up joint arrangements rather than the less tangible ingredients that make partnership successful. Partnership work is not something that can be confined to some parts of an organisation. Every part of the organisation, including support services, finance, personnel etc should have an understanding of the culture of partnership and the need to behave differently.

Dr Walid El Ansari, Lecturer in Public Health at Wolverhampton University, was part of a thee year study of five Community Partnerships in Health in post- apartheid South Africa. Findings from the study led to some conclusions and lessons for successful partnership in any setting. The key principles identified were:

> **Agreed mission, goals and outcomes.** Understanding about why different partners need each other to solve problems and improve outcomes for people. Agreement about short and longer-term goals

> **Clarity about:** objectives, roles, procedures, expectations, rules, responsibilities, commitment

> **The importance of relationships.** Time spent on building mutual trust, respect and long-term commitment. Qualities such as patience, tolerance, persistence, willingness to share, open-mindedness, respecting other people's sensitivities

> **Effective communication.** Finding a common language. Developing feedback loops to avoid misunderstanding. Ensuring that all partners have an equal voice. Sharing the same information, at the same time, through clear lines of communication

> **Leadership.** Leaders who are skilled and visible. Recognition that skills may vary as partnership moves from initiation to implementation to routine management

> **Consultative decision-making.** Wide consultation and decision-making that is not perceived as being made by a small inner circle. Respecting different views and avoiding tokenism

> **Setting realistic timescales for action**

Some people who use services, carers and staff might be forgiven for a lapse into hollow laughter at this point at the prospect of the large and powerful agencies that they have to deal with or are employed by, acting in these enlightened ways. Others will have a more positive view and will be aware that people are trying very hard to achieve this kind of culture and way of working and some are succeeding.

None of this is easy and it is likely to be a slow and time-consuming process if it is to succeed.

ORGANISATION DEVELOPMENT AND CHANGE MANAGEMENT

It is helpful to have a strategy to help staff embrace partnership as part of an organisation development programme. This should be an integral part of partnership arrangements from the beginning, rather than an afterthought.

Some of the change process will happen constructively as a result of the energy and drive of individuals. If it is to be sustained and more universally adopted, a staff and organisation development and change management programme will need to be in place.

A development programme will involve:

- a planned approach
- the use of skilled trainers
- tapping into the skills and experience of those who have been engaged in partnership work
- willingness to explore these areas reflectively and with constructive feedback on how people are behaving in the change process.

There are a number of approaches to organisation development and change management, and some organisations will already have developed their own way of managing this. Some approaches rely on the planks of re-organisation, the replacement of staff and new training in the hope that they will produce the intended change. However, as Gerald Smale points out in *Managing change through innovation (National Institute for Social Work, 1998)*,[18] some approaches to change *'actually precipitate consequences that are opposite to the intentions'*. Examples of this might be the introduction of a decentralised structure that ends up decreasing local autonomy or the development of 'needs-led' assessment processes that end up being more service-led than the practice they replaced.

Smale points out that current management theory (eg *Mintzberg, 1989*,[19] *Peters and Waterman, 1982*,[20] *Senge, 1990*,[21] *Kotter, 1996*,[22] *Kanter, 1985*[23]) suggests that an organisation that manages change and innovation well is characterised by open communication, with flatter structures *'that blur the formal distinctions between people but also up and down and advocate replacing formal structures with a shared understanding of and commitment to the organisation's vision'*. In this kind of environment new ideas and ways of working happen through a process of *convergence of thinking* rather than *coercion*. These ideas recognise the complexity of any change process and the need to understand the position of all the people involved, asking questions like '**Who has to think and make judgments about what?**' Smale describes how different approaches may be needed within the same change process, where for example, people may be acting as creative autonomous individuals, but also be required to produce some standardised performance.

> *'When behaviour has to be synchronised, standardised, uniform, it can be directed by a single chain of command. Where behaviour has to be constantly changing to meet changing circumstances on the ground, then the ever changing patterns of behaviour can only be maintained by co-ordinated individual judgements acting under broad policy directives. The co-ordination of these actions is itself in the hands of practitioners, each of whom judges what to do based on the constant observation of terrain and colleagues' actions and each has to be capable of taking command of the situation if required.' (Smale G, 1998[18])*

This means that the change management approach should fit the task and be adapted as appropriate to match what people actually need to do in practice. This requires some active thinking and planning that involves everyone concerned.

Smale proposes an approach based on the notion of constantly asking '*Who sees what as a problem?*, to be clear about '*What needs to change?*' and equally to give importance to the question '*What needs to stay the same?*'

Dealing with these questions involves overlapping strands of activity, represented in the diagram overleaf by interconnecting triangles.

The inner triangle represents the process of identifying *What changes and what stays the same?* Time is given at this stage to work with different people to get a view of what needs to happen where. Change doesn't happen tidily and not everything will need to change. This is an opportunity to check with people *Who sees what as a problem?*

The next triangle shows how managers can use this information to plan change by:

- Mapping the people – who are the key and significant players? What sort of change needs to happen with different key people to bring about change?
- Analysing the change in order to plan action and timescales to match different people and circumstances: How complex is it? What are the

Change management – an ongoing process

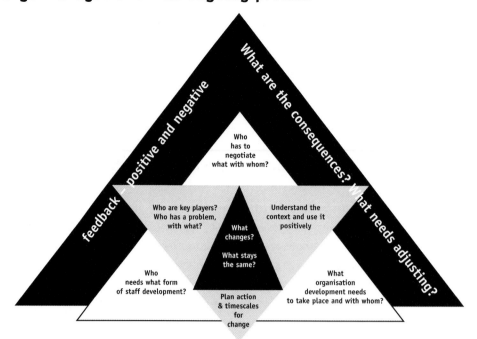

resource implications? What rules and policies need to change? What are the likely timescales for different parts of the change process? Who will now need to make what decisions?

- Understanding the context of the change and using it to the advantage of the change process: What's going on in the organisation? The wider political context? What will work for and against change?

The timing of this is key. Organisations sometimes leave the change management plan until too late in the process, or consider it only after the change has actually taken place. It helps considerably if people are clear about how the change process will be managed before it actually starts happening.

The third triangle represents the stage where the negotiations that need to happen take place and staff training and organisation development plans are mapped out.

The outer triangle indicates that this is a dynamic rather than a step-by-step linear process. Activity will be happening at all levels and sometimes with feedback that takes the organsation back a stage, for example to do more work on staff development with a specific group of staff.

Bringing about change

Once the change management plan is set, this model advocates five modes of organisation development:

- Consciousness raising events
- Training in skills and aspects of service delivery

- Team building
- Workshops on joint working
- Developing relationships.

Consciousness raising events

These are opportunities to present and illustrate new ideas and approaches. They are likely to influence people who are responsive to change and will probably not have much influence on others. They are nevertheless important in engaging opinion leaders and champions for change. Change will not happen as a result of these events but they will lay the ground for change.

Training events and staff development

Short courses and skills workshops of a few days' length or in a longer term training plan will provide training in specific skills and knowledge and innovation.

A programme focusing on partnership will need to include work on **key skills and attitudes** such as:

Sharing	Negotiating skills	Flexibility
Openness and honesty	Influencing without	Courage to compromise
Constructive argument	controlling	Changing the balance of power
Confronting difficulties	Networking	Understanding the difficulties
positively	Patience and persistence	of joint working and how
Leadership	Creativity	to minimize them
Developing a learning culture	Observing and giving	
Listening and balancing views	constructive feedback	

Team building/inter-disciplinary work

These activities look explicitly at how people relate to each other, how tasks can be shared and constructive ways of working together.

Looking at the culture of organisations

These activities focus on looking at the current culture in organisations and what might need to change in culture and attitudes to meet new objectives.

PROMOTING A LEARNING CULTURE

A learning organisation is able to consider in a healthy way what has been done well and and what has gone wrong. Learning from good practice and innovation requires an organisational environment which, for example, has developed:

- Good communication that tells people about good practice and helps people make important links

- Processes for actively promoting changes in practice through specific training programmes
- Ways of encouraging considered and planned innovation and risk taking.

Learning from things which have not gone well is an altogether more sensitive and difficult process. A recent publication *An organisation with a memory (DoH, 2000)*[24] reports on the findings of an expert group that was set up to examine how the NHS could more effectively learn lessons from failures in clinical care. The report makes the point that even when things go seriously wrong, important lessons may not be learned. This can be due to a range of factors, for example, the existence of a culture which seeks to attach blame to individuals when things go wrong, rather than encouraging an open examination of the context which allowed the mistake to happen.

The report recommends that, in order to learn from failure, development needs to take place in four key areas:

- Unified mechanisms for reporting and analysis when things go wrong
- A more open culture, in which errors or service failures can be reported and discussed
- Mechanisms for ensuring that, where lessons are identified, the necessary changes are put into practice
- A much wider appreciation of the value of the system approach in preventing, analysing and learning from errors.

The report also outlines specific action needed to create these conditions.

An example of a reporting mechanism can be found in Appendix 4. It gives a format for highlighting the area to be considered, describing what was intended, what actually happened, what lessons could be learned and what action is needed to ensure that learning takes place and any necessary changes are brought about. The introduction of a simple process like this in a non-threatening way could make a real difference to how people can learn positively from the consequences of decisions and actions.

Talk to people and help them understand what change is proposed and why it is needed

Listen to people and get their views on the broader consequences of change and also how it will affect them and their work specifically

Ask people what needs to change and what needs to stay the same in the broader context and specifically for their area of work

Think about who the key players are and where they stand

Consider what will work for and against the change process

Use all this information to develop a change management plan that matches the complexity of the change needed

Make sure the change management plan is timely and happens in advance of some of the signals of change (eg before job interviews for re-structuring take place)

Get feedback from people (including those outside the organisation) about the consequences of change and continue to adjust actions and plans in response to this

Promote and develop a learning culture

6. WORKING IN PARTNERSHIP FOR PERFORMANCE MONITORING AND REVIEW

The idea of active performance monitoring and quality assurance has been with us for some time now. In practice, however, it is still sometimes a process that is not very well thought through and is an afterthought rather than a key and everyday part of the management process. *Facing the facts (DoH, 1999)*[11] reports that only 11 out of 21 authorities in the study had a formal process for evaluating the quality of current services. Only 10 out of 21 authorities reported a joint and systematic process for consulting service users and carers. The study also revealed little evidence of effective quality assurance processes between commissioners and providers.

There are a number of ways in which performance monitoring and review will need to be further developed, for example:

- National standards and performance frameworks
- Charters, rights and statements about what people can expect
- Best Value
- Clinical Governance
- Inspection and regulation
- Accreditation
- Complaints procedures.

Individual organisations, or parts of organisations, cannot monitor the achievement of the required standards or aims and objectives by themselves. Each of these areas should involve a partnership approach with service users and carers and key stakeholders. People can be involved in a variety of ways (see Chapter 3 *Developing a joint strategy and joint plans*) in drawing up standards and measures and in the process of evaluating, monitoring and inspecting. Ken Simons' book *A Place at the Table?* (*BILD, 1999*)[7] also describes some ways in which people can be involved in all of these processes.

It may be helpful to draw up a **Performance Plan for Partnership** that can be put together in partnership with all stakeholders and which outlines how, in each of the processes, in each organisation and jointly, people will be involved. The areas the plan might cover could be, for example:

- National Standards and Performance Frameworks
- Charter, rights and expectations
- Best value
- Clinical governance
- Inspection and regulation
- Accreditation
- Complaints procedures

National standards and performance frameworks

There were five areas for development identified in Facing the Facts:

☞ **Policy guidance to confirm the direction of strategic change**
☞ **National objectives for health and social care services for people with learning disabilities are needed, together with targets for achievement in the medium term**
☞ **Information about the local achievement of national objectives and targets**
☞ **A set of service standards and an effective means of regulation**
☞ **Further development of inter-agency approaches to planning and commissioning services.**

The *Performance Plan* will need to indicate how this will happen locally.

Charters, rights and expectations

It is helpful to have public statements about rights and expectations, eg:

- In general terms about services
- In relation to advocacy
- With regard to access to information that helps decision making
- About entitlements
- About what should happen in accessing and receiving services
- About how people can participate.

These should be drawn up with the involvement of people using services and their families and in full consultation with all stakeholders.

Best Value

Best Value is a system of local authority purchasing that replaces compulsory competitive tendering with a process that is intended to take account of the quality of services as well as costs. The principles of Best Value require local authorities to carry out a programme of reviews of all their services over a five year period.

Reviews are based on four strands of activity:

- Challenging – Why and how is a service provided and is it needed?
- Comparing – Checking out performance against other services, local authorities, organisations etc
- Consulting – With people using services and all stakeholders
- Competing – Looking at alternatives and options to ensure the most efficient and effective services.

The emphasis placed on consultation in the Best Value Review process provides an opportunity to involve people with learning disabilities and their families at all stages, for example:

- Deciding which areas should be reviewed
- Defining the scope of the review
- Designing the review and the methods and tools to be used
- Deciding on recommendations for action
- Implementing action from reviews.

Clinical Governance

Clinical Governance: Quality in the New NHS (*Department of Health, 1999*)[27] introduces the process of clinical governance to the NHS.

> **'It takes a developmental approach, focusing on the fundamental shift required to enable good clinical quality. The vision emphasises the need for a move to a culture of learnng – an open and participative culture in which education, research and sharing of good practice thrive.' (Chief Medical Officer 1999)[28]**

Ways in which people with learning disabilities and their families can be involved could be:

- As part of any feedback from quality programmes
- By developing more accessible and responsive complaints procedures
- People are able to contribute to evidence base by reporting their view on the effectiveness of the treatment or help they have been given.

Inspection and regulation

Formal regulation for residential care services is carried out through inspection and registration of homes. People can be involved in the process:

- by being consulted during inspection
- by being trained to become 'lay members' to be part of the inspection team
- by participating in advisory panels that each inspection unit is required to set up.

Accreditation

There are a number of ways in which services can be externally looked at and accredited. Schemes such as Investors in People and British Standards offer organisations a chance to measure themselves against externally determined standards. *The Quality Network*,[26] for example, is a scheme which has been developed specifically for services for people with learning disabilities. The scheme has been jointly developed by The British Institute of Learning Disabilities and the National Development Team.

The process is centred around a review, leading to an action plan. The process is supported by an external nationally appointed 'Quality Coach'. The approach concentrates on improving outcomes for people using services by working alongside and involving people with learning disabilities, their families, staff and key local people. It involves spending time with people and getting close to their experience of services. The service is monitored against a core set of outcomes:

- ☞ I make everyday choices
- ☞ People treat me with respect
- ☞ I take part in everyday activities
- ☞ I have friendships and relationships
- ☞ I am part of my local community
- ☞ I get the chance to work
- ☞ I take part in important decisions
- ☞ People listen to my family's views
- ☞ I am safe from harassment and abuse
- ☞ I get help to stay healthy

The monitoring tools to measure services against these outcomes are designed so that they are accessible for people with learning disabilities to use (see Appendix 5).

Complaints procedures

Complaints procedures give people a way of making services more responsive to their needs if they have been unable to achieve this in any other way. Processes for complaining can be difficult for people with learning disabilities to use. Involving people with learning disabilities in the design of the process and in ways of promoting it, such as videos and photo-packs, will help give them a greater understanding of their rights and how to exercise them.

SUMMARY

Identify the areas in which monitoring and evaluating need to be happening

Work with all stakeholders on how people can be involved in all the processes

Draw up a *Performance Plan* so that people can see how they can be involved in all the areas of monitoring and evaluation

Whatever the organisational arrangements, partnership working is not easy. It requires some careful thought and planning but it is an art and also requires sensitivity and creativity. It will require people to do things differently.

The most important partners are people with learning disabilities and their families. The biggest partnership challenge is to make them central in all areas of planning, implementation, assessment and care management, the provision of services, review, inspection and quality monitoring.

No matter how much agreements may be bound up in written agreements and structures, success will ultimately rely on good relationships built on mutual trust. If these are absent the first job is to think about how good relationships can be developed.

Good relationships depend on spending time together to talk things through. Time for this needs to be built in. Sometimes independent facilitators can help to move things on.

Wherever people are, and whatever is going on elsewhere, people can demonstrate good practice in their own attitudes, behaviour and ways of working. The combination of individual behaviours can produce a critical mass that can eventually have a strong influence.

Joint plans are needed to give a framework and direction for partnership work. These will take time to develop if they are to be the true reflection of good consultation and involvement of all stakeholders.

Community Teams will need to have a clear focus and be able to demonstrate the positive difference they can make in people's lives. They will need to help develop and adapt to a person-centred approach.

A change management plan will be needed to ensure that organisations are ready to embrace new ways of working. This should be developed in a timely way and should not be an afterthought when key elements of change have already taken place.

REFERENCES

1. Department of Health (1998) *Partnership in Action (New opportunities for joint working between health and social services): A discussion document.* London: Department of Health.

2. Department of Health (1997) *The new NHS: Modern, Dependable.* London: Department of Health.

3. Department of Health (1995) *Practical guidance on joint commissioning.* London: Department of Health.

4. Department of Health (1999) *Modernising Social Services.* London: Department of Health.

5. Department of Health (2000) *Guidance on the Health Act Section 31 Partnership Arrangements.* London: Department of Health.

6. Ovretveit J (1993) *Co-ordinating community care: Multi-disciplinary teams and care management.* Buckingham: Open University Press.

7. Simons K (1999) *A Place at the Table?* Kidderminster: British Institute of Learning Disabilities.

8. Craft A (1996) *Abuse of younger and older people: similarities and differences* in *the abuse of care in residential institutions.* London: Whiting and Birch, SCA Education.

9. Greig R and Peck E (1999) *Is there a future for the community learning disabilities team?* Tizard Learning Disability Review Vol 3 Issue 1.

10. O'Brien J (1987) *A guide to personal futures planning* in Bellamy T G, Wilcox B eds *A comprehensive guide to the activities catalogue. An alternative curriculum for youths and adults with severe learning disabilities.* Baltimore: MD Paul H Brookes.

11. Department of Health (1999) *Facing the facts: Services for people with learning disabilities. A policy impact study of social care and health services.* London: Department of Health.

12. Social Services Inspectorate (1998) *Moving into the mainstream: The report of a national inspection of services for adults with learning Disabilities.* London: Department of Health.

13. Smull M and Harrison B (1992) *Supporting people with severe reputations in the community.* Alexandria, VA National Association of State Directors of Developmental Disabilities Inc.

14. Wertheimer A, editor (1995) *Circles of support building inclusive communities.* Bristol: Circles Network.

15. Whittaker A and McIntosh B (March 2000) *Changing days.* British Journal of Learning Disabilities Vol 28 No 1.

16. NHS Executive (1998) *Signposts for success in commissioning and providing health services for people with learning disabilities.* Wetherby: Department of Health, NHSE.

17. NHS Executive (1999) *Once a day.* London: Department of Health, NHSE.

18. Smale G (1998) *Managing change through innovation.* London: National Institute for Social Work.

19. Mintzberg H (1989) *Mintzberg on management: inside our strange world of organisations.* New York: The Free Press.

20. Peters T and Waterman R H (1982) *In search of excellence: lessons from America's best run companies.* New York: Doubleday.

21. Senge P M (1990) *The fifth discipline: The art and practice of the learning organisation.* New York: Doubleday.

22. Kotter J P (1996) *Leading change.* Boston: Harvard Business School Press.

23. Moss-Kanter, R (1985) *Change Masters: Corporate entrepreneurs at work.* London: Allen and Unwin.

24. Department of Health (2000) *An organisation with a memory: Report of an expert group on learning from adverse events in the NHS*. London: Department of Health.

25. Greig R, Cambridge P, Rucker L (1996) *Care Management and Joint Commissioning* in *Purchasing Services for people with learning disabilities, challenging behaviour and mental health needs*. Kidderminster: British Institute of Learning Disabilities.

26. The Quality Network, contact: Sharon Powell. Telephone: 01562 850251.

27. Department of Health (1999) *Clinical Governance: Quality in the New NHS (HSC 1999/065)*. London: Department of Health.

28. Chief Medical Officer (1999) *CMO's update 22: Clinical Governance*. London: Department of Health.

29. Department of Health (2000) *Joint Investment Plans: A learning disabilities workbook*. London: Department of Health.

30. Department of Health (2001) *Valuing People: A new strategy for learning disability for the 21st century*. London: Department of Health.

31. Department of Health (2000) The NHS Plan: *A Plan for Investment, a Plan for Reform*. London: Department of Health.

APPENDIX 1

PRESENTATION MATERIAL

What do people with learning disabilities want and need in the 21st century?

I get help to:

- Take part in everyday activities

- Get and keep a job

- Stay healthy

- Have friendships and relationships

- Live independently

To achieve these outcomes joint working is essential

- *Can't do this as single agencies*

- *Find ways of working together*

  - joint commissioning?
  - joint plans?
  - aligned budgets/pooled budget?
  - integrated provision?
  - agreed priorities
  - joint purchasing?

With

- Have to go all over the place for services
- Budgets in different agencies
- Tensions about who should provide what
- Fragile – held together by goodwill
- Energy spent on holding things together

Without

- Services brought together
- Single budget with one budget manager
- Staff recruited according to need
- Stable arrangement with stable resourcing
- Energy spent on getting the service right

Why bother?

Provides a good tool to achieve objectives

- More flexibility
- More stability
- Quicker response to need
- More cost effective
- Better services that people want

SELF-ASSESSMENT

Developed by Ace, a self-advocacy organisation using 'The Change Picture Bank'

Ace
c/o Saxmundham Centre
Seaman Avenue
Saxmundham
IP17 1DZ

My Assessment

Please write your name here:

An assessment is when Health and Social Services finds out what support and help people want and need.

They do this by talking to people with learning difficulties themselves and to other people who are important in their lives.

This form is for you to fill in by yourself or with someone you trust.

It gives you a chance to say what support you think you need to live the life you would like to.

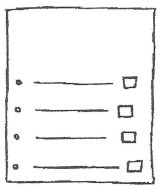

Please tell us about your life now.

Where do you live?

Who do you live with?

What do you do in the day?

What are the good things you do in the day?

What would you change about what you do in the day?

What do you do in the evenings?

Any hobbies or interests?

What else would you like to do?

What do you do at weekends?

Any hobbies or interests?

What else would you like to do?

What support and help do you get now from other people? e.g. family, friends, staff

Have there been any changes in your life that you would like to talk about?

Is there anything else you would like to talk about? e.g.

- where you were born
- which school you went to and what you liked
- where you have lived in the past
- any jobs you have had
- do you believe in any religion
- which language do you speak
- anything else about your way of life?

What would you like to do? e.g.

- live more independently
- move house
- find work
- make more friends and relationships
- go to college
- think about what I do in the day

What help and support do you need?

To help you to do the things you have talked about, the person doing your assessment will look at different areas of your life.

Please tick the areas you would like your assessment to look at:

- ➢ Where you live------ ☐
- ➢ Work or education--- ☐
- ➢ Money---- ☐
- ➢ Personal care-- ☐
- ➢ Medication and treatment-- ☐
- ➢ Sensory abilities e.g. hearing, sight--- ☐
- ➢ How to get on with other people-- ☐
- ➢ Things you do in the day--- ☐
- ➢ Health--- ☐
- ➢ Learning new things--- ☐
- ➢ Mobility or getting about--- ☐
- ➢ Communication skills-- ☐
- ➢ Family and other relationships-- ☐

I would also like my assessment to look at:

Thank you for filling in this form.

Please can you sign it here:

Signature: _____

Date: _____

George Lewis
27.11.99

If someone has helped you to fill this form in,
could they fill in this part. Thank you.

Name: _____

Relationship: _____

Signature: _____

Date: _____

FRAMEWORK FOR REVIEWING MULTI-DISCIPLINARY WORKING

This framework is not comprehensive but it provides a checklist for some of the ingredients for effective multi-disciplinary working. You can add questions to this to make it more detailed or locally relevant.

For each section, work in your team to look at:

a) What happens now and what needs to change?

b) What issues need resolving and how can they be resolved? What will help?

c) What action needs to be taken, by whom and when?

1. REFERRAL

- ❏ Where do referrals come from?
- ❏ Who responds, how and how soon? Is there a 'reception process' where people receive an initial response and details are taken? Does this also involve a single source for basic information and advice?
- ❏ Is there standard documentation for receiving and recording referrals?
- ❏ Are referrals logged across disciplines in a single system?
- ❏ Is referral information collated to give a picture of what is coming in to the team? Have you agreed what information would be useful to collect and collate?
- ❏ Is there an agreed style and approach and standards about how the team responds (ie what experience do people have when contacting the team – Accessible? Helpful? Polite? Respectful? Informative? Prompt? etc). Is this monitored with feedback?

2. ALLOCATION

- ❏ How is work accepted for allocation? Who is responsible for doing this?
- ❏ Is there a team meeting? How frequently? Who attends? Is this respected and accepted as a process for the whole team? If not, what needs to happen to ensure collective responsibility?
- ❏ What criteria are used?
- ❏ What happens if referrals are not accepted for allocation?
- ❏ How are people referred on to other services if the team does not accept them for allocation?

3. ASSESSMENT

- ❏ If more than one professional is involved, how is the work co-ordinated?
- ❏ Is there an agreed format for assessment which uses core information?

- ❏ Is there agreement about a person-centred approach? Are there opportunities for the person referred and/or their carer/advocate to record what their expectations are, their view of the help they would like and what outcomes they would like?
- ❏ Do people have an opportunity for self-assessment?
- ❏ Is there a co-ordinated Health Action Plan?
- ❏ How does a Health Action Plan link in with a Community Care Plan?

4. RECORDING

- ❏ Is there a joint recording system with core information?
- ❏ Is there a single system for checking who is involved from the team?
- ❏ Is there a single data base? What information needs to be on the data base? Who has access to it? Who is responsible for putting information onto the data base?
- ❏ How are outcomes measured?
- ❏ How is this audited?
- ❏ Do people with learning disabilities hold their own records?

5. SUPPORTING OTHERS IN THEIR WORK

- ❏ What percentage of the team's work does this involve? Does the balance need to change? How will an action plan for this be drawn up?
- ❏ Are team members clear about what this work involves? Is there a training need for the team? How will this be met?
- ❏ How are people with learning disabilities helped to access mainstream health services? Does the balance need to change?
- ❏ How are general health outcomes measured as a result of specialist support in health promotion and accessing mainstream health care?

6. INTERVENTION

- ❏ How are agreed care programmes and interventions co-ordinated?
- ❏ Who takes responsibility for this?
- ❏ What systems support joint work?
- ❏ Is the balance of intervention and other work right? Does this need to change?

7. REVIEW

- ❏ What is the review process?
- ❏ How are reviews co-ordinated within the team and with other agencies, providers ete?

- ❏ How are people with learning disabilities, carers or advocates made central to this process? Does this need to change?

8. CLOSURE

- ❏ What is the process for closing cases?
- ❏ How is this recorded and by whom?

9. MONITORING, QUALITY ASSURANCE, CLINICAL GOVERNANCE

- ❏ How does the team measure its effectiveness?
- ❏ How are people using services and their families involved in this?
- ❏ What outcome measures are there?
- ❏ Are there agreed standards and performance measures?
- ❏ Who is responsible for what in the monitoring process?
- ❏ Who takes the lead in clinical governance? How is it being managed and monitored?

10. RELATIONSHIPS

How good are relationships? Try this exercise with individual team members, if necessary anonymously and then as a team. What can you learn from what needs to change?

In the team?

- ❏ To what extent do people co-operate within the team?

Very little co-operation				Good co-operation
1	2	3	4	5

- ❏ How open and honest are people able to be with one another?

Communication not very open				Open communication
1	2	3	4	5

- ❏ Do people trust one another?

Low level of trust				High level of trust
1	2	3	4	5

With people outside the team?

(Make a list of key partners, including people with learning disabilities and their families) For each of them ask:

❑ To what extent do people co-operate with people outside the team?

Very little co-operation   Good co-operation

1	2	3	4	5

❑ How open and honest are people able to be with people outside the team?

Communication not very open   Open communication

1	2	3	4	5

❑ Do people trust others outside the team?

Low level of trust   High level of trust

1	2	3	4	5

APPENDIX 4

SHARED LEARNING

PARTNERSHIP WORKING
FRAMEWORK FOR DISCUSSION TO ASSIST SHARED LEARNING

It is helpful if people are able to learn from experience in a way that does not avoid dealing with difficulties, but that isn't simply about trying to apportion blame. In this process, everyone accepts a collective responsibility to help work through what happened when something went wrong, or when it was an example of good practice. The aim is to agree on action that can be taken by all concerned to improve or maintain practice.

AREA FOR DISCUSSION

> *(This is just a one-liner to describe the general area for discussion eg joint decision making, responsibility for funding, co-ordination of work, communication etc)*

ISSUE

> *(This should describe the area for discussion in more detail eg describing the background to work with an individual, outlining the area of confusion over funding, describing the process for communication etc)*

WHAT HAPPENED?

> *(This should tell the story as simply as possible eg describing what happened after a decision had been made. At this stage there should be no attempt to explain, just to record the facts. For example, It was agreed at a multi-disciplinary meeting that the key worker from the residential service would work with a Community Nurse to support X in his wish to remain in his work placement. This involved planned work with X at home and with the employer at the work placement. The work did not take place and the work placement broke down. Or – a decision was made by managers at one level about the allocation of funding to create new posts. Work took place to set up the posts and recruit to them. The decision was overturned at a higher level at a later stage.)*

WHAT ASSUMPTIONS WERE MADE?

> *(This should outline what assumptions people were making eg about delegated authority, about responsibility for action etc)*

WHAT OUTCOMES ARE DESIRED?

(This should describe what the desired outcome from the learning process would be eg reliable communication systems, clarity about delegated authority, maintain an area of good practice and extend it across a service etc)

LEARNING QUESTIONS?

(What constructive questions do you need to ask about what happened?)

For example:

- ❑ Was there lack of clarity about processes for decision making?
- ❑ What was the quality of partnership working in the process?
- ❑ Where are the strengths and weaknesses in the communication system?
- ❑ How could we have done this in a more effective way?

CONCLUSIONS

(This should describe the conclusions you can agree on about what happened and what needs to happen)

ACTION NEEDED TO ADDRESS THE CONCLUSIONS

(This should record the action agreed to address the conclusions based on the shared learning)

APPENDIX **5**

QUALITY NETWORK OUTCOME MEASURES (CHOICE)

Sample recording sheet

1 I make everyday choices

Ratings	★ ★ ★ ★ ★	★ ★ ★ ★	★ ★ ★	★ ★	★
		✓			

Evidence What we found out	Source Person Observation Family member Documents Staff Other
Makes herself a drink whenever she wants one	Observation
The TV was on for the whole of my visit switched to ITV, with no-one watching much of the time.	Observation
Staff asked (name) if she wanted lunch, she chose to wait until later	Observation
Staff ask when she wants to eat - she decides	Staff
(Name) is given a choice of clothes to wear every morning	Staff
Guidelines have been written to help staff involve (name) in activities and make choices	Documents
There were few activities to choose from for (name) to do at home	Observation
(Name) decides when to get up and when to go to bed	Staff

The Quality Network

Working in partnership with other organisations and agencies can be a complex, sometimes fraught process. Yet the rewards for making a partnership work can be immense.

This guide is for anyone in learning disability services about to embark on joint working, or looking for ways to improve their current practices.
Drawing on case studies and experiences of successes and failures, the guide looks at the realities of partnership working, including:

- **Working towards partnership**
- **The different kinds of partnership arrangements**
- **Developing a Joint Investment Plan**
- **Partnership work with people with learning disabilities, and their families**
- **The ingredients of a successful partnership**
- **Maintaining quality standards.**

About the author

Anita Cameron is County Commissioning Manager (Specialist Services) in Suffolk. This post is part of a Joint Commissioning Team which brings together the planning and strategic commissioning functions of Suffolk Social Services and the NHS relating to community and mental health services. Anita's areas of responsibility include services for people with learning disabilities.

ISBN 1-902519-64-7

9 781902 519647

Design: Fiona Keating
Print: Latimer Trend & Company Ltd